Flute

How to Use the CD Accompaniment:

A melody cue appears on the right channel only. If your CD player has a balance adjustment, you can adjust the volume of the melody by turning down the right channel.

ISBN 0-7935-8456-6

HAL•LEONARD®
CORPORATION
7777 W. BLUEMOUND RD. P.O. BOX 13819 MILWAUKEE, WI 53213

Visit Hal Leonard Online at
www.halleonard.com

CONTENTS

WE WILL ROCK YOU ◆1

(Recorded by QUEEN)

Words and Music by
BRIAN MAY

Flute

WILD THING ❷
(Recorded by THE TROGGS)

Words and Music by
CHIP TAYLOR

Flute

Lower notes optional

DANGER ZONE ◆❸
(from the Motion Picture TOP GUN)

Words and Music by
GIORGIO MORODER and TOM WHITLOCK

Flute

ROCK & ROLL-PART II ◆4
(The Hey Song)

Words and Music by
GARY GLITTER and MIKE LEANDER

Flute

MCA music publishing

8

TWIST AND SHOUT ◆ ⑤
(Recorded by THE BEATLES)

Words and Music by
BERT RUSSELL and PHIL MEDLEY

Flute

BORN TO BE WILD ◆❻
(Recorded by STEPPENWOLF)

Words and Music by
MARS BONFIRE

Flute

MCA music publishing

FINAL COUNTDOWN ◆7

Words and Music by
JOEY TEMPEST

Flute

I GOT YOU ◆8
(I Feel Good)

Flute

Words and Music by
JAMES BROWN

DEVIL WITH THE BLUE DRESS ◆9

Flute

Words and Music by
WILLIAM STEVENSON and FREDERICK LONG

Pumpin' Rock

GONNA MAKE YOU SWEAT 〈10〉
(Everybody Dance Now)

Words and Music by
ROBERT CLIVILLES and FREDERICK B. WILLIAMS

Flute

Y.M.C.A. 11

(Recorded by THE VILLAGE PEOPLE)

Words and Music by JACQUES MORALI,
HENRI BELOLO and VICTOR WILLIS

Flute

GET READY FOR THIS ◆12◆
(Recorded by 2 UNLIMITED)

By JEAN PAUL DE COSTER,
FILIP DE WILDE and SIMON HARRIS

Flute

PLAY MORE OF YOUR FAVORITE SONGS
WITH GREAT INSTRUMENTAL FOLIOS FROM HAL LEONARD

Best of the Beatles
89 of the greatest songs from the legends of Liverpool, including: All You Need Is Love • And I Love Her • The Fool on the Hill • Got to Get You into My Life • Here, There, and Everywhere • Let It Be • Norwegian Wood • Something • Ticket to Ride • and more.

00847217	Flute	$9.95
00847218	Clarinet	$9.95
00847219	Alto Sax	$9.95
00847220	Trumpet	$9.95
00847221	Trombone	$9.95

Broadway Showstoppers
47 incredible selections from over 25 shows. Songs include: All I Ask of You • Cabaret • Camelot • Climb Ev'ry Mountain • Comedy Tonight • Don't Cry for Me Argentina • Hello, Dolly! • I Dreamed a Dream • Maria • Memory • Oklahoma! • Seventy-Six Trombones • and many more!

08721339	Flute	$6.95
08721340	Bb Clarinet	$6.95
08721341	Eb Alto Sax	$6.95
08721342	Bb Trumpet/Bb Tenor Sax	$6.95
08721343	Trombone (Bass Clef Instruments)	$6.95

Choice Jazz Standards
30 songs, including: All the Things You Are • A Foggy Day • The Girl From Ipanema • Just in Time • My Funny Valentine • Quiet Nights of Quiet Stars • Smoke Gets in Your Eyes • Watch What Happens • and many more.

00850276	Flute	$5.95
00850275	Clarinet	$5.95
00850274	Alto Sax	$5.95
00850273	Trumpet	$5.95
00850272	Trombone	$5.95

Classic Rock & Roll
31 songs, including: Blue Suede Shoes • Blueberry Hill • Dream Lover • I Want to Hold Your Hand • The Shoop Shoop Song • Surfin' U.S.A. • and many others.

00850248	Flute	$5.95
00850249	Clarinet	$5.95
00850250	Alto Sax	$5.95
00850251	Trumpet	$5.95
00850252	Trombone	$5.95

The Definitive Jazz Collection
88 songs, including: Ain't Misbehavin' • All the Things You Are • Birdland • Body and Soul • A Foggy Day • Girl From Ipanema • Love for Sale • Mercy, Mercy, Mercy • Moonlight in Vermont • Night and Day • Skylark • Stormy Weather • and more.

08721673	Flute	$9.95
08721674	Clarinet	$9.95
08721675	Alto Sax	$9.95
08721676	Trumpet	$9.95
08721677	Trombone	$9.95

Latin Gold
16 Latin favorites, including: Bésame Mucho • Brazil • Evil Ways • The Girl from Ipanema • Granada • Malaguena • Mas Que Nada • One Note Samba • Perfidia • Quiet Nights of Quiet Stars (Corcovado) • Sama De Orfeu • So Nice (Summer Samba) • Tico Tico • and more.

00841461	Flute	$5.95
00841462	Clarinet	$5.95
00841463	Alto Sax	$5.95
00841464	Tenor Sax	$5.95
00841465	Trumpet	$5.95
00841466	French Horn	$5.95
00841467	Trombone	$5.95

Disney's The Lion King
5 fun solos for students from Disney's blockbuster. Includes: Can You Feel the Love Tonight • Circle of Life • Hakuna Matata • I Just Can't Wait to Be King • Be Prepared.

00849949	Flute	$5.95
00849950	Clarinet	$5.95
00849951	Alto Sax	$5.95
00849952	Trumpet	$5.95
00849953	Trombone	$5.95
00849003	Easy Violin	$5.95
00849004	Viola	$5.95
00849005	Cello	$5.95
00849955	Piano Accompaniment	$10.95

Best of Andrew Lloyd Webber
26 of his best, including: All I Ask of You • Close Every Door • Don't Cry for Me Argentina • I Don't Know How to Love Him • Love Changes Everything • Memory • and more.

00849939	Flute	$6.95
00849940	Clarinet	$6.95
00849941	Trumpet	$6.95
00849942	Alto Sax	$6.95
00849943	Trombone	$6.95
00849015	Violin	$6.95

BOOK/CD PLAY-ALONG PACKS

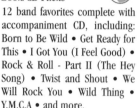

Band Jam
Book/CD Packs
12 band favorites complete with accompaniment CD, including: Born to Be Wild • Get Ready for This • I Got You (I Feel Good) • Rock & Roll - Part II (The Hey Song) • Twist and Shout • We Will Rock You • Wild Thing • Y.M.C.A • and more.

00841232	Flute	$10.95
00841233	Clarinet	$10.95
00841234	Alto Sax	$10.95
00841235	Trumpet	$10.95
00841236	Horn	$10.95
00841237	Trombone	$10.95
00841238	Violin	$10.95

Movie & TV Themes
Book/CD Packs
12 favorite themes, including: A Whole New World • Where Everybody Knows Your Name • Moon River • Theme from Schindler's List • Theme from Star Trek® • You Must Love Me • and more.

00841452	Flute	$10.95
00841453	Clarinet	$10.95
00841454	Alto Sax	$10.95
00841455	Tenor Sax	$10.95
00841456	Trumpet	$10.95
00841457	Trombone	$10.95
00841458	Violin	$10.95

Praise and Worship Solos
Book/CD Packs
15 favorites, including: Blessed Be the Name • Come, Thou Fount of Every Blessing • Holy, Holy, Holy • I Stand Amazed in the Presence • Rejoice Ye Pure in Heart • To God Be the Glory • more.

00841373	Flute	$12.95
00841375	Alto Sax	$12.95
00841376	Clarinet/Tenor Sax	$12.95
00841377	Trumpet	$12.95
00841378	French Horn	$12.95
00841379	Trombone	$12.95

My Heart Will Go On
Instrumental Solo Book/CD Pack
This arrangement of Celine Dion's mega-hit features a solo part for instrumentalists to play with a real orchestral background that sounds exactly like the original!

00841308	Solo for Flute, Clarinet, Alto Sax, Tenor Sax, Trumpet, Horn or Trombone	$6.95
00841309	Solo for Violin, Viola or Cello	$6.95

0400